Magic for sure. Golden everlasting magic. I love how his mind works and I want to see the nimbus. I suspect Pauline is not the only one that adores Jack. It seems we all do. He is quite remarkable.

Deirdre Wallace
Relationship therapist and teacher in the UK

Pauline Daniel discovered she was spending "quality time" with Jack in a way that she hadn't done with her son. Freed from the anxiety of constant parenting, she felt as if her appreciation of precious moments was heightened . . .

Of course, there are billions of grandmothers—and probably more than a few grandfathers—who might have considered [writing] a similar memoir. But, as Daniel will be the first to tell you, there is only one Jack.

The result is a nice little book, modest but true, by an observant grandmother who happens to live in British Columbia.

Alan Twigg
BC Bookworld

Anyone who has ever loved a child will appreciate Pauline Daniel's generous sharing of her love for her grandson Jack. Readers will also appreciate the wisdom of innocence that punctuates every chapter of this book, "Jackisms" recorded by "Buba" every Tuesday of Jack's early years. *Tuesdays with Jack* is a testament to the simple joys of seeing the world as a child again.

Cathy Sosnowsky
author of *Holding On: Poems for Alex*
and *Snapshots: A Story of Love, Loss and Life*

The love in this beautiful little book just pings off the pages. It's a great read!

Rae Naka

In Pauline's book, I felt the deep love that women, in particular, hold for their children and grandchildren. Moments of my own childhood washed over me in a mixture of joy and reverence.

Marci Loukianoff

I hope you laugh out
loud ~ cry a little bit
~ feel all the Love!

Tuesdays with Jack

Pauline ♡

Tuesdays with Jack

a grandmother's love and a little boy's brilliance

Pauline Daniel

GRANVILLE ISLAND
PUBLISHING

ISBN 978-1-926991-82-5 (paperback)
ISBN 978-1-926991-90-0 (ebook)

Book editor: Chantel Hamilton
Book designer: Shannon Eyben
Photography: Jim Fenning

Granville Island Publishing Ltd.
212 – 1656 Duranleau St.,
Vancouver, BC, Canada V6H 3S4
604-688-0320 / 1-877-688-0320
info@granvilleislandpublishing.com
www.granvilleislandpublishing.com

To Jack, the little love of my life.

You astound me!

Contents

Foreword

If you are a grandmother or want to be one, this little book will amuse you and touch your heart. It will remind you of your own childhood and early years of parenting. Pauline writes as if you are sitting in her kitchen chatting over a cup of tea. I smiled as I read and continued to smile with each page. And you don't just read this book; you listen to it.

If you are lucky, you can read this book in one sitting, immerse yourself in its warmth and humour, and then sit back wrapped in your own memories. Then look forward to the next magical visit with your grandchildren because, as Pauline Daniel says, when we are with our grandchildren "our hearts are fully engaged and we are being who we really are."

In this beautiful book, so tenderly illustrated, you will learn that despite your grandparents' and parents' failings and because of their indelible spirits, you have absorbed the best of them while taking your own path to parenthood. You may have avoided some of their pitfalls and fallen into others, but when you look into the mirror you will see them, and—oh no!—hear them too. Pauline shares her wisdom and experiences openly and with candour, and the love in every word is irresistible.

"Memories are time travel," Pauline says, and I enjoyed every one. Umbrella strollers, blue baby carriages that double as day beds, and carriage returns on our typewriters—I remember it all and felt right at home in each chapter! How my grandmother friends are going to enjoy this book.

Leslie Gibbons
author of *A Fairy Tale for Mothers*

Introduction

Becoming Buba

God, you have blessed me indeed, as the
child I love has had a child I love with all
that is within me.

Jane Craft, "A Grandparent's Prayer"

Shawn said, "You're going to be Buba, right?"

I hadn't thought of myself as Buba, and I'm not sure why. I
assumed I'd be Grandma. Buba was special to Shawn because he
had one and wanted me to be one, too.

A few weeks later, I was at a barbecue gathering. It was almost
the right time, and I called my son and daughter-in-law to ask
permission to share their news with some of my family. It was
my news, too. They said yes!

And then it was out in the open. My heart was full of love and a new energy. It was definitely time for a baby in our family.

I noticed a woman about my age with her daughter, grandchildren, and a new baby. They were having a picnic at the park. She was happy, present and laughing as she held the baby, played with the other children, and supported her daughter. She was easy with it all. It was a lovely little glimpse into her life. She was the poster for baby-boomer grandmothers.

Part of me was just a smidge disappointed at letting go of having a granddaughter. The other part was incredibly happy. I know little boys.

Yahoo! Soon I could start buying for this little guy! But they quickly had what they wanted and needed. They researched everything, went totally natural, and bought a combination of new and used online.

It was fun for me to revisit little baby boy things. At our local consignment store, I bought a Tupperware toy Shawn had had as a baby, little toy cars and trucks, a few bits of clothing, and, of course, books. I washed, softened, folded, and disinfected it all. Waiting . . .

Jack came into the world in the spring of 2011. I loved him from the time he was a thought. Most things I can anticipate, but becoming a grandmother wasn't one of them. It just blew me away.

I wasn't prepared—in the same way that nine months of pregnancy doesn't actually prepare you for motherhood—for the all-encompassing, unconditional, flesh-of-my-flesh love I felt for that baby—instantly.

Grandmother. Grand mother! So special. My son's son. My baby's baby. All of this symbolism magnified the love in my heart. I couldn't wait to see him, hold him, and smell his little head.

He was home within a few hours of his birth. Amazing. The first time I saw him was on my computer screen, and I just sat there gazing at him, tears streaming down my face.

My daughter-in-law's mother travelled from England to help and support her. I knew that wasn't my place, and I didn't want to intrude. I just wanted to see and hold that baby while he was still brand new. It was so important to me.

We had made plans for a quick trip to have our first visit. The night before we were to leave, Shawn called to tell me that everyone was still trying to settle in, and that it might be too stressful to have me over so soon.

It was a blow and a crushing disappointment to feel we would be imposing. This was also an uncomfortable a-ha moment, knowing how hard this call was for my son. He was caught between his mom and his wife.

I promised we would only stay for a few minutes. Just long enough to meet Jack and give him a cuddle. We wouldn't impose. We would be there just to meet Jack. However brief, I would take it.

I was bursting with love and adoration and could hardly contain it. Sitting with it until they were ready as a family for me to share it was agony. I, too, had arrived at a new place in my life.

It was a lonely start. I think mothers of sons experience this more often, and we walk a fine line. We don't fit in the same way that a mother's mother does. And I felt like an outsider peeking in. Where was my place?

It wasn't the first time I'd experienced this feeling. When Jack's parents got married, I was acutely aware of being the mother-in-law. I watched.

When we arrived to meet the baby, I was excited but timid. He was wearing a little red sleeper and we posed for photos, both grandmothers taking turns holding Jack.

I remember holding Shawn as a brand new baby—totally in love and at the same time realizing, *Oh my god! This is forever!* None of that fear, overwhelm, or enormous sense of responsibility was there for me as a grandmother. The love was as pure as it gets.

We had lunch, a short visit, and a cuddle with the baby. And then we left. The next morning, we had another little cuddle before the seven-and-a-half-hour drive home. It was so hard to leave my boy and his boy. I can only imagine what my daughter-in-law's mother felt leaving when she returned to England.

The best part was knowing they would soon be moving to my town, where they'd decided to buy a house, live and raise their family. It was here waiting for them, and so was I . . .

Still, it wasn't an easy transition. I felt I was imposing most of the time when I really just wanted time to be with the baby. I asked too often and probably came on too strong. I don't think they wanted me to be this way, so hell-bent. When Jack was about six or seven months old, I was told no other grandmother in their circle of friends was like me.

It was true that I wanted to be with the baby more than with his parents. And maybe they thought I had abandoned my mothering role. Or maybe they didn't think of me at all. I was running on instinct and heart. It was such a big new role. It overtook me.

Slowly, and bit by bit, I was allowed in. Taking Jack for walks in his stroller was like walking on air. I swear the joy in me splashed everyone around us. A woman I know said, "I watched you with Jack. I don't think your feet touched the ground. I could feel your energy from across the street."

I am blessed and lucky that they live nearby and that I could be part of their daycare system. By now they knew how much I wanted to be Buba and have regular time with Jack. Frankly, I think I wore them down.

I spent Tuesdays with Jack from the time he was a baby until he started kindergarten.

It was wonderful to rock him to sleep and to sing the same songs I sang to his father. (My voice was better then.) Changing "nappies," playing, and being with Jack in a way I hadn't with my son. More free, totally present and having fun. It's still that way when we are together. I think it's an anti-aging formula.

My son wanted me to be Buba because everyone should have one. In my life, bubas spoke Russian. They knew stories, poems, and special songs. They could knit, quilt, make soup from anything, and turn a dried lump of cracked cheddar into flaky biscuits.

That's not quite me. I'm a buba who works out, is self-employed, dances to country music, and loves her jeans.

Reading in a swing, one-pot meals, and laughing are some of my favourite things.

Now, Buba is part of my soul. It opens my heart.

Jack and Buba

Gymnastics class

"What was that song I was singing, Buba? I ran out of batteries in my head so I guess I runned out of songs."

"Your brain ran out of batteries?"

"Only for songs, nothing else."

Jack, age 4

My grandmother had five grandchildren. She called us by each other's names. She was a young grandmother, so she wasn't confused—our names just didn't come up fast enough. And then she laughed. If she was going to scold us, it was gone in her laughter.

She laughed at herself. What a gift. She was the most important woman in my life, and I still miss her. I understand her laughter and where it comes from because these days, it's happening to me.

Jack and I are at gymnastics, an activity we have scheduled for Tuesday afternoons. It's a busy place. A huge room filled with trampolines, balance beams and bars. Kids of all ages are running, jumping, and swinging on the equipment. It's non-stop for ninety minutes, and Jack expects me to keep up and watch his every move. Sometimes, I admit, I'm watching the clock.

A woman leans over to ask me Jack's name. I say Shawn (that's his dad's name), and then quickly correct myself: "No, no, no, his name is Jack."

Where did my mind go? It must have "runned" out of batteries for names, that's for sure, including my grandson's.

The woman looks at me as if I am slightly bonkers. She probably wonders if Jack is safe with me or if I am actually his grandparent.

I am shocked and amazed that my brain can switch in that way. The colour of Jack's hair, the shape of his head, the way he runs. It's Shawn. My brain and my heart love, see, and know two children, and it happens in a flash. I am my grandmother. The moments are fused.

There's a holy sacredness in this experience, and that's why laughter is so appropriate—even though others may think we're off our rockers.

It's a grandmother moment. Not to be analyzed or diagnosed, but appreciated and enjoyed. Let's laugh. There's no language for this.

Jack's right: sometimes our brains just run out of batteries.

What's that floppy bit?

"How strong are your muscles, Buba?"
I proudly flex my bicep.
"What's that floppy bit?"

Jack, age 3

Seeing Jack, before I first held him, made me want to live for a long, long time. It was a message from deep in my soul. And when that happens, you pay attention.

I knew I needed to be fit, healthy, and strong. But I'm not athletic. Reading in a swing, away from bugs, is more my style.

So, what did I do? I joined a CrossFit gym. Probably one of the most challenging, intimidating, and downright scary things I've ever done. But I felt encouraged by Jack's mum and my personal trainer, who told me that *anyone* can do this. They assured me the program is scalable to fit you. I nodded, remembering how much fun aerobics classes used to be.

It was January, the middle of winter, and Chloe was picking me up for my first 5:30 a.m. CrossFit class. I'm a morning person, but this felt more like the middle of the night.

I walked in . . .

This is not aerobics.

Rap music was blaring. People were *jumping* onto high boxes. They were swinging kettle bells above their heads (I didn't know what a kettle bell was until right then). They were squatting with weighted bars on their shoulders. There was a bucket of powdered chalk in the middle of the floor.

The class was full. There were a few young junior Leafs hockey players in the group, and I recognized two city police officers. Most of the women were half my age. There wasn't another grandmother in sight.

I made my way to the back of the gym, wondering if I should make a run for it. But I didn't. My deep desire to be strong and fit motivated me. Surviving the class was my focus and I hoped I could walk out of there intact.

I stayed for three years and showed up three times a week until it wasn't so intimidating anymore. Those high-intensity, heart-pumping, endurance-testing workouts started to change the way I looked, felt, and moved in my body.

And in a funny daydream, I now hear myself say, "Oh, wait a second, Jack, Buba will just *jump* up there and get that for you."

Focus on the muscle, not the floppy bit.

You look old

"Buba, do you have an extra chin like Grandpa?"

"Buba, you look old."
"Old? No, I think I'm beautiful."
"Yes, you're beautiful, Buba, but you look old."

Jack, age 5

Jack examines me. We can be cuddled up with his books on my feather quilt, or together in my easy chair finding hidden pictures in his magazines. He notices my face, my words, my laughter, and points out very clearly what he sees and hears.

At five years old, he has no filter. His innocence is so pure and profound, it pierces my heart. And in an instant, I'm laughing and crying at once. I appreciate its truth, and I wish it could be this way forever.

Seeing things the way they really are can be jarring and hard to accept. But when we do, it's freeing. And what I'm saying is, I see my mother in myself.

I realize it when I catch a glimpse of my ears in the mirror one morning. They're huge! They are old lady ears. They are my mother's ears. How could this be, and how long have they been this big, and can other people see how big they are?

Unless they keep growing, I think I can hide my ears. But other parts of my mother are showing up in me now, too. I can hear inflections of her voice in mine. I see both of us in my face. It catches me off guard. I'm not sure I like it.

And in the last few months, I've started saying "oy." That makes me and Jack laugh.

I was listening to a conversation in my family and noticed myself leaning forward, with my elbow on my knee and my chin in my hand. My mom used to sit that way, and as I did it, I swear I could feel her. It was as if she was in me looking out. Moments like this surprise me, and I don't fully understand them. But they help me understand her.

There's a richness and a depth to aging that's lost when I focus on my chins and neck (mine looks like ET's) and floppy bits. Jack can see beauty and age as one.

Women Make It Happen

My favourite buba

"You're my favourite buba."

Jack, age 3

Jack has just turned three. The kids (Jack and his mum and dad) are over for dinner. For dessert, I've made an apple and pear crisp, a never-fail *Canadian Living* recipe from the '80s, only now I use organic fruit and very little sugar. Of course, I still top it with soft mounds of real whipped cream.

Jack has never tasted whipped cream. He is standing on a chair at the end of my kitchen counter helping me whip it. His little hands are on top of mine, and together we are holding my vintage Black & Decker mixer.

Cream is splattering all over my kitchen wall, onto our faces and hair, and we are laughing over the sound of the beaters ricocheting off the the sides of the bowl.

It's time to serve the apple crisp. Jack takes a big spoonful of the whipped cream and looks at me in a dreamy little state and says, "You're my favourite buba."

It is instantly the best compliment I have *ever* received. I want to hold him close but dare not disturb his moment of bliss.

How can I possibly ever make whipped cream without Jack? It would feel wrong. This is our memory—*our thing*.

We still make whipped cream together, and Buba serves it on almost every dessert.

Always busy

"Buba, Grandpa said, 'Buba is always doing something busy.' "

"Thank Buba and Grandpa for all your Christmas presents, Jack."
He gives me a big hug.
"And Grandpa, too, Jack."
"Buba did it all."

Jack, age 4

My grandmother could grow anything. She spent all summer outside in her enormous vegetable garden and with her prize-winning flowers. She wore overalls, a big hat, and no bra. She made the best bread. I remember her kneading and shaping the loaves and bouncing the dough off our faces before putting them into the pans to bake. And laughing.

She also had her seed catalogues. She spent winter planning her gardens and teaching us the Latin names for all her flowers. She loved the seasons and told us magical Russian stories. She made patterns in frost come alive.

We loved when Bub (short for Bubushka) would do her spring cleaning. It was a madhouse. She didn't start in one room or in one place. She took the whole house apart and let us make forts with sheets and spin on the floor with lids from old pots. We helped shine the floors by sliding on them in big woolen socks after she had put wax on them. Way more fun than the floor polisher.

My mom, too, rarely sat still. She stood at the kitchen counter, wiping, peeling, chopping, visiting, and generally giving orders. I loved her cooking and baking. I've never tasted better shortbread than my mother's. She appreciated a good apron, and wore them all of the time. One still hangs on my pantry door.

Mom was a master multi-tasker. When she finally sat down in her favourite chair, she was surrounded by her projects. Knitting baskets with needles, big safety pins, and hooks sticking out of them; notepads with lists; an emery board for a quick manicure; half a cup of cold coffee; and books. She always had more than one on the go. (Except for the knitting needles, this describes me, too!)

There was love and magic in the purposeful clutter around my mother. Out of it came the most beautiful creations—always perfect for the people she gave them to.

When my son was five or six, he loved all things Star Wars and asked his Buba to make him a Star Wars sweater. What would my mom know or care about Star Wars? Nothing. But she loved and cared deeply for Shawn, and in a few weeks, a parcel arrived just for him. My mom had designed an original pattern, bought just the perfect shade of blue yarn, and knit him a sweater with a Snow Walker on the front. He lived in it.

I can't do that—any of that. I buy things. And work hard at making lists of ideas for just the right gifts. I'm both my mom and her mom. In the kitchen, my grandmother did things by feel, and she was okay with loose ends. She cooked everything together in an electric frying pan. My mother could put the finishing touches on anything, including a holiday.

One time, Jack wanted a knight-in-shining-armour suit and a magician's outfit so badly that he started asking, almost pleading with me, weeks before Christmas. I made sure they were bought and tucked away, hoping he wouldn't change his mind.

When the day finally arrived, he opened his knight suit, and I heard him say, "This is actually beautiful!" He came to Christmas dinner in his magician's sparkly red vest, cape, and top hat. Perfect.

Mum will know

Reading Jack a bedtime story in his room, I notice that he has picked his nose.

"What are you going to do with that?"

"I'll ask Mum. She'll know."

Jack, age 4

Women are tuned in. I've never forgotten Marlo Thomas saying that a woman must have radar attached to her uterus so she can find the missing things. And don't we?

We know our family's schedule, children's needs, how many toilet paper rolls are under the bathroom sink, and the meaning of every sound in our home.

We know when things are humming along as they should or about to fall apart. And this includes the lives of the people we love and hold dear.

One of the many wondrous things about women is that we have a relationship with *everything*—our cars, household appliances, favourite perfume, collection of scarves, and, of course, our shoes.

When my husband semi-retired and we no longer needed two vehicles, I sold mine. It was my first brand new car, and I loved it. There she was, all white and shiny, just waiting to be sold to me. I wanted a white car because my business logo would look great on it. And it did—people knew my car.

As I drove it to its new owner, I said my final teary goodbyes. I told it how thankful I was that even on the coldest winter morning I could count on it to start. I thanked it for the freedom it gave and for helping me market my business.

As I was expressing my appreciation, I could sense my car letting me know that selling it was a good thing, that it needed to be driven more and to be of greater service.

These things amaze my husband. Actually, I think it freaks him out a little bit, that I can walk into the kitchen and know when food is cooked perfectly and ready to be taken out of the oven. Or that I can smell when rice is done or just about to burn. If he cooked a little more often, I know he could develop this magic, too.

We anticipate things in our lives and in others' lives, on many levels and from all perspectives. I know you know what I mean. Then we plot, plan, and prepare for every eventuality—usually as we lay our heads on our pillows. It's how we grow the eyes in the back of our head.

When my son was learning to talk, he said "Mommy" all day long. *All day long.* Is it bedtime yet? He said Mommy when he wanted something, when he didn't want something, when he was tired, hungry, or happy. Mommy meant everything.

As a young teen, "Mommy" became "Hey, Mom." When he started with "Hey, Mom," I knew something was coming, and I could usually tell what each "Hey, Mom" meant. He wanted Mom to drive him somewhere or pick him up from somewhere. He wanted permission to do something, food, and the big one—money.

Once when Shawn was late coming home on a school night and I was pacing the floor in that place between anger and fear that parents know so well, in he came through the door. And before I could say a word he said, "I know you're worried and angry, Mom. I'm late because I've just seen the best movie, Mom, and you've just got to see it, too."

The next day, I shared that story with a friend and she said to me, "If your teenage son thinks *Forrest Gump* is the best movie he's ever seen, his values are in the right place, and you have nothing to worry about."

I should have known. Usually, I do. It's that radar thing again. And I'm happy that when I hear "Hey, Mom" these days, it usually means "Will you take Jack for a sleepover so we can have a date night?"

It's all your fault

"I'm going to put you in a dungeon, Buba."

Jack, age 2

"This is your fault, Buba."
"What's my fault?"
"Everything!"

Jack, age 4

Let's admit, being 100 percent responsible for your life just sucks sometimes. It's so much easier to blame others for everything, or to just take the blame and feel sorry for yourself. Either way, you're off the hook. I know, I did both. Had I been taught to live from that basic truth, I would have been in the front seat of my life much sooner.

It took me forty years to get it. I think that's what "Life begins at forty" means. There's an energy in that decade, and I felt it coming for a couple of years. It was magic, and it filled me up with myself. That's when I knew I couldn't put off making some big, scary changes any longer. Life would be much, much better in the long run, for me and my son, without my cigarettes and my first husband.

When I quit smoking, my son said it was the best birthday present I could give him. I don't know if I'll ever get over that guilt. And when I told my mom that my decision to leave my marriage came shortly after I had quit smoking, she said "Well, of course. All the smoke cleared." And then she added, "Just stay mad!"

That was her way of helping me get out, and stay out, of an unhealthy marriage. Over the years, I've shared her advice with many other women who also understood it as soon as they heard it.

In my marriage, only my husband could be angry, in a bullying, I-am-the-boss kind of way. My mom's three little words changed all that. Now I let myself feel my own anger and act on it. Like pulling back the curtain in the old *Wizard of Oz* movie to cut through his bluster and expose truth.

Those three little words were a gift from my mom. They made me feel brave and strong like a warrior; they took me out of a war zone; they made me feel defiant and free, and I took up swearing (I think that's why women and kids like it so much). I learned anger is righteous and very grown up.

Sadly, most women are conditioned, in one way or another, to hide our anger under a sweet smile. I still cringe if I'm told I'm sweet. I remember how uncomfortable people were to ask me how I was after my marriage ended. I think they were hesitant because I might actually display my anger...and then what? You'd think I was waving a gun.

Two-year-old Jack wanted to put me in a dungeon because I wouldn't play London Bridge Is Falling Down over and over and over for him. I understood his anger and where it came from. He was seriously ticked with Buba, and he let me know it.

Jack and I share a flair for drama, so I was very impressed with the way he articulated his anger and level of frustration. He was very clear: he wanted nothing more to do with me. Not laughing is the hard part.

He was easier to distract and calm when he was two. At four, when something went wrong with his art project, or anything else, he blamed me. He wanted to lash out—there was so much raw emotion, and it splashed all over Buba. *That's okay, Sweetie,* I thought. *There's a lot going on right now. I can take it.*

We go over to the feelings chart on my wall, where there are faces showing mad, sad, happy, and afraid. We pick one, act it out, laugh, and learn. Phew—this day, it worked.

This is what learning to be responsible and in the driver's seat looks like when you're four.

High-Tech Tools, Low-Tech Buba

Not your buba's stroller

Buba, age 60-ish

I brought my baby home from the hospital in my arms. Just walked out the door with him. No rear-facing car seat required. We had an unsecured, portable travel bed that was basically a plastic box with some padding on the inside. I doubt it would pass any safety standards now. And yes, I loved my baby.

Ours was the generation that brought natural childbirth and breastfeeding back, introduced prenatal classes, and insisted on dads in the delivery room. And it was more common to see pregnant women working. Where I worked, there were two of us expecting babies within a month of each other.

It was great. Brenda and I read all the new books, compared notes, and supported each other to eat healthy, but I have to admit, we started having the occasional cheeseburger at about the time our babies' brains were developing. And there was nothing sexy about our ever-expanding breasts getting in the way of the carriage return on our typewriter. (You may have to google *carriage return*—we still had one relic in the office.)

I had five dozen cloth diapers with bunny rabbit pins, neatly folded and ready for my baby, but then a friend gave me a box of newborn Pampers. This was a modern high-tech convenience before *landfill* was part of my vocabulary.

When Jack was a baby, I just had to buy him a bright green Bumbo baby seat. It was adorable, way too expensive, and probably something they could easily have lived without. We didn't have anything comparable for Shawn. I used a retro plastic baby seat from the '60s that had been sitting in my aunt's basement for fourteen years.

Shawn was fussy one Saturday evening, and nothing would soothe him. I decided to strap him into the little seat and put him on the floor—*yes*, in front of the TV. *Hockey Night in Canada* was on, and I thought he might like all the action on the screen.

Somehow, in his excitement, and in a split second, he managed to tip himself over, face first with the little seat still on his back. Poor baby. I was horrified, guilt ridden, and thankful for the green shag carpet.

One of my favourite things was the beautiful blue baby carriage that my coworkers gave me. It doubled as a daybed, and when we went out for walks, my baby faced me so I could talk to him and see his sweet little face taking in the world around him. I missed that with Jack. I had to peer around the front of his stroller to see his face.

Umbrella strollers were new and popular for toddlers in the late '70s. I think mine cost $26.00 at Woolworth's. With a tap of your foot, it would fold or unfold. It took up very little space, and it really did hang on your arm like an umbrella. Great for bus rides. There was absolutely *nothing* complicated about my umbrella stroller.

Now Jack's stroller was a super-duper deluxe model that you could run over rugged terrain with or roll effortlessly along city streets while still having room for your latte—but it needed a series of lessons to use.

I asked the kids (Jack's mum and dad) to leave the stroller upright when they brought it into my house on Tuesday mornings. That way I didn't have to wrestle with it to take Jack out for his sleepytime walks.

Putting the stroller into my car on my own was a giant pain, and it reminded me of cramming Shawn's fancy bike into my hatchback when he was a teen. It scratched and gouged the finish in my car and left black tire marks on everything.

After errands one Tuesday, I was feeling extra confident. I flicked my wrist in just the right way and pressed all the red levers on the stroller—but nothing happened. I did it again and again, over and over, but the stroller would not collapse. Two-year-old Jack was antsy in his car seat, and people were starting to watch Buba struggle with the stroller. It baffled even the people who stopped and tried to help.

Eventually, I gave up and called Jack's mum. She left work and walked to my car to rescue us. In a couple of minutes and with great finesse, she had the stroller collapsed and neatly stowed in my car. Phew. (Maybe I just needed to drink more water.)

Don't press anything

"Buba, I've done this a million times with
Grandpa. Don't press anything."

Jack, age 5

Grandpa told Jack he could use his iPad while he was out.
This was a very big deal. They usually do puzzles, draw, or
play games together.

I just wanted a closer look to see what Jack was doing. But it
seemed that even my vibration could cause disaster.

At first I wanted to laugh, and then . . . wait a minute . . . this
didn't feel good. I was being put in my place. It stung, and it
was uncomfortable on many levels.

This transported me. Memories are time travel.

I put my grandmother in this place once too many times. She
helped raise me. It was necessary, incredibly special, and very
hard as a kid, having divided loyalties.

It was the evening of my big Christmas concert at Tarry's
Elementary. Our little country school put on the most

amazing events for the community, and this concert may have been the biggest.

The costumes were elaborate, and my grandmother pulled out all the stops. She took my mom's satin wedding gown apart, dyed it blue, and, on her treadle sewing machine, turned it into a Victorian bustle dress for me to wear. I loved it.

My grandfather had gone to pick up my mother from her last shift at work. She was a nurse. It was just me and my grandmother, and she was trying her best to do my hair. It wasn't working. I hated it, and I wanted my mom to be there to do it right.

I was convinced that my grandmother didn't know what she was doing, that because of her, everything would be ruined, and in this heightened state, I lashed out at her and let her know that it was my mom who got things right—that my mom knew just what to do and she would fix this as soon as she got there. And I was much older than Jack. I mean, really, it wasn't long after this that I was a Beatles fan.

To this day, I am so sorry that I may have hurt her. She laughed, but I wonder what she did with those feelings. A reckoning for me now.

"Buba, don't press anything," is my full-circle moment, and it speaks volumes. Jack is protecting something special with his grandpa; I'm wondering if he really thinks I could destroy it.

Siri

Jack asked Siri, "How did you make my mummy and daddy so special . . . and how did you make my buba and grandpa so special?"

Jack, age 3

Does it get any better than Facetime calls? For long-distance grandparenting, this is a godsend. Talking to Jack while he's in the bathtub and we're at the Safeway parking lot with our groceries still amazes me.

When Jack says, "Just ask your phone, Buba," I feel like I'm in a *Jetsons* cartoon. My family didn't have a TV or a phone until I was twelve. Now I'm texting, googling, and connecting with Facebook friends all over the world. It's a high-tech version of penpals from Grade 5.

But this is where I'm caught: somewhere between the fun stuff and the never-ending learning curve. It's frustrating, and it wears me down. It doesn't always make sense. It can take me half an hour to update my monthly calendar, only to discover that we both need the car at the same time on the same day. Really, do I need to take full responsibility for this because the settings on my iPad weren't on Share?

You know what I miss? Just turning on the TV. Is *radio* still a word? How many universal remotes does it take to watch your favourite show? I keep mine in a basket that I have to keep upgrading to hold them all.

Today's technology pushes all my buttons. It taps into the fear that I can't learn and stay current and so will be left behind. It questions my values, and I do my best not to be swept up in the discombobulating speed of life.

And then this happened.

It was Sunday morning and Jack had slept over. He was cuddling with Grandpa. They were playing on his iPad and he was introducing Jack to Siri. I was nearby, flipping through the newspaper, when I saw Jim waving his arms in the air mouthing, "Write this down, write this down!"

Jack was speaking to Siri. He was asking how she made his mummy and daddy so special, and then he included us, wanting to know how Siri made Buba and Grandpa so special.

OMG. We were dumbfounded, mouths open. What a sweet and precious moment we were witness to: this little three-year-old's love and appreciation for his family.

A remarkable juxtaposition.

Bittersweet Guilt

Doing it differently

Buba, age 60-ish

Chloe is the mum I wanted to be, and Shawn is the dad he didn't have. This makes me proud and happy. I must have done something right.

My hopes and dreams for parenting and raising Shawn didn't always match my reality, and I filled that gap with great gobs of guilt over the years. The biggest hurt was that I quickly became a single parent in a two-parent home.

I think it's universal—mother love and mother guilt. Did I really do the best I could, or is that just an excuse to hide behind? It's probably pointless to ponder and time to put the bashing stick down, lay it to rest in the past where it belongs. Are you listening?

Life now is what matters most. I see how happy and secure Jack is. He has so many people who love and adore him, and he knows it. He has a good life. I never worry about him.

I wish my grandparents could have said the same thing. But no, they worried endlessly. My parents were teenagers when I was born, and my dad drank—not a good combo. Their drama, and there was plenty of it, overshadowed my needs most of the time.

My grandparents were still a young couple, under forty. Can you imagine? They didn't even have a break. They just stepped in, bless them, and helped raise me and my brother. They were everything to us and made a lonely start into a beautiful childhood. They gave us a secure and stable home where we always felt safe and warm.

I was twenty-six when my son was born. In 1978, that was considered older for a first baby. Older, but not necessarily smarter. The desire to have a baby was stronger than my plan for becoming a mother. And nine months of pregnancy didn't change that.

In my daydreams, I had a guitar and sang to my baby in a field of flowers, like Joan Baez. In my reality, I had an unsupportive husband. It was like having two babies, and the older one was more demanding.

The expectation was that I would put the baby down, get back into my jeans and have dinner ready, cinnamon buns in the oven, and generally never miss a beat. And I tried.

I'd read all the books and had gone to all the classes. I was older and could handle it, and that's what I told my mom when she offered to help. Oh, was I wrong. Of course, my mother knew better and insisted on coming a few weeks after Shawn was born.

By that time, he had shown me how tough a cranky little newborn could be. When my mom walked through the door, her arms were open, and I just handed him to her.

Shawn's crankiness didn't go away, and my mom was concerned, too. My doctor's office paid attention when they heard it was the grandmother who was calling and not a hysterical new mother.

We were seen by a new, young doctor. I had some trouble with my thyroid during pregnancy, and his theory was that my milk was being affected and probably the cause for Shawn's upset. To be sure, he ordered blood tests. A horrible ordeal.

In the end, it remained a theory and I began supplementing with formula. A few major disappointments within weeks of becoming a new mother.

My mom was forty-five—a young grandmother, too, with loads of energy. Grandmother love took over, and she was ready to be mother and grandmother. She was a much better buba than she was a mother. I hope Shawn *never* says that about me.

I was fifty-nine when Jack was born. Ancient compared to my grandmother and my mother. I am so very grateful for this amazing experience, and can't imagine life in my sixties without Jack.

Yes, I have regrets, and yes, I'd like a few do-overs. Don't we all? But it is what it is. I think I finally understand what that little phrase means. It's an acceptance of life so far. And some of it is bittersweet. That's what love and age will do. The joy and the sadness mixes and jumbles up into one, great big, beautiful moment called Now!

My Christmas tree looks different

Jack, ages 4 and 5

When Jack leaves at the end of the day, my Christmas tree looks different. The bows and some of the decorations around the fireplace mantel have been rearranged and are now on the tree. In my mom days, I would have fixed it. As Buba, I leave it, and feel joy and a deep peace that is new to me.

Believe me, this is growth. Back in the day, inner peace meant order, things in their place, lined up and matching. Neat rows of labelled ice cream buckets for Shawn's Legos, little cars, and crayons were always easy to find. Soup with soup and beans with beans in my pantry; cup handles facing the same way in my kitchen. Still, my mom could never put things back the way I had them arranged.

So you can imagine the discomfort I felt when a silver ornament or little red bow was out of place on my Christmas tree. I'm not a totally laid-back buba yet but maybe a mellowed version of my younger self. Good thing, because I used to clean with toothpicks and Q-tips. I know . . . who else does that? That's why hiring someone to clean my house doesn't work.

I have to believe that it wasn't all a waste of time, that somehow Pledge and Pine-Sol brought me to this moment. To the wonder and delight of being someone's grandmother.

It's December, my favourite month of the year. Jack helped pick out our tree. He and I are getting ready to decorate it. Layers and layers of memories and bittersweet feelings are flooding me as we unwrap the paper-plate wreaths and garlands Shawn made in school and the precious salt-dough Santas we made together when he was four.

There is so much wrapped up in Christmas. Jack loves hearing the stories attached to all the ornaments his dad grew up with and made. I think I did the best I could, making memories and magic for Shawn in spite of his "Bah, humbug" dad.

The tree is loaded with every decoration I own, and Jack has made a new tree topper. "Buba, that glitter [tinsel]— I *love* it!" Me too, and more goes on. As we decorate, we step back to admire our work. Then we stand at the front door to see how beautiful the tree and the mantel are when you first walk in. Jack likes this, and I'm sure that's what has led to the redecorating of the little red bows.

I laugh. I cry a little bit. Pour a glass of lip-smacking red wine, light my Himalayan salt-light candle, and count my blessings.

Jack's accident

Jack, age 4

It was the perfect start to a good old-fashioned winter day. In the morning, Jack and I painted bright flowers in the snow with food colouring and built a twisty snow maze under the elderberries in the backyard.

To make it extra special and a bit scary for his mum, Jack put his jungle "aminals" in the corners of the maze and added big drops of red paint along its curvy path. He was a zombie at Hallowe'en, and we still have some of that energy going on here.

After lunch, the two of us set off to do some sledding, and Jack takes his snow shovel so we can make jumps. "Your job is to dig, Buba, and mine is to test it out." Hmmm . . . sounds like a plan, Jack.

On the way to the hill, I carried his shovel and dragged his saucer sled. We held hands and talked about anything and everything. There was wood smoke in the air, and it reminded Jack of a bonfire at my brother's, where he made us hot dogs and

marshmallows. "The outside of the marshmallow is like crispy bread, Buba, and the inside is gooey. I love the gooey part."

Me too, Jack.

We were at the top of the hill later, ready to leave for home, when Jack decided to do a run on his own, head first. It caught me off guard, and as I turned to look, he began to spin out of control. He was going too fast, and he was too far down the the hill for me to do anything but watch. I was horrified and almost frozen in fear. I saw what was about to happen.

And then it did.

His head hit a cement abutment and bounced off. Oh my God, oh my God. I was so afraid. He lifted his head and started to cry. I barrelled down the hill, thinking that if he was crying, he was okay.

His lip was cut and instantly swollen, there was some blood, his teeth were intact, and his helmet was still on his head. Again, thank God, thank God. I just held him.

He was in shock. So was I, as we started our walk home together. He was still crying, and that was just what I wanted to do, too. I kept telling him he was okay, and I was going to call his mum and dad as soon as we got home.

When we finally walked through the door, I carefully took off his helmet and snow gear, and I noticed a huge bump on his forehead, scratches on his face and neck. His lip was even bigger now. And . . . I had to call his mother.

I talked to Chloe and explained what just happened. She reached Shawn, and to reassure her, he reminded her that his mom worries about everything. I said yes, while some of that is true, I thought Jack needed to see a doctor. Chloe agreed and came for him early. Jack was so happy to see his mum.

I was still feeling guilty because this happened when he was with me. If he had been Shawn, I would have had only the one layer of mother guilt. I think only children are an experiment the whole way through, and that's why I was an overprotective mom.

Jack was seen immediately at the walk-in clinic, and after his examination, they called to let me know that he was fine. Great news; I was relieved. He was okay—I was not. I still felt guilt-ridden, and my mind kept seeing him spiraling out of control on the hill. Over and over in my head . . . until the next evening when they FaceTimed me and Jack said, "Buba, my lip's gone down, and I have a new haircut!"

Jack, like every Canadian kid, will have scary sledding experiences. Too bad this one had to happen with his buba.

Power of Play

Imagination

Jack, ages 3, 4, and 5

In my life, play was something you did as a child and grew out of quickly. At ten or eleven, I badly wanted a Barbie, but my grandmother told me I was too old for more dolls. Barbie was kind of the end for me.

There was no value or benefit attached to play. And adults definitely weren't involved. Sure, they threw a ball around every so often or they coloured, but that was about it.

Play was a way to deal with children, or not to deal with children, and to get them out of the way. *Oh, just go play. Just go play outside.* Being sent outside was hell for me. I was an only child for six years. Adults were my company. Outside meant alone, and I spent way too much time there. I think it's why I'm a shy extrovert and don't like bugs.

I received mixed messages about play, and they came from my grandfather. Work was way more important to him, and there was always work to be done. The women in my family worked hard, too. They just had more fun in them, and I loved when they were all around. It was freeing.

My grandfather was more serious, and when my outgoing, noisy, high-energy self came out, it disrupted him, and he would tell me to *just settle down*. That became a theme for me.

This way of being is what I brought to motherhood. Oh, my poor boy. I must have been such a boring mother. I made sure he had everything he wanted. I stood on wet soccer fields when he was five, in stinky karate dojos when he was seven, in ice-cold hockey arenas when he was twelve, and at the bottom of mountains where he came flying down on his bike in his teens. He could always count on me being there, but I feel tremendous guilt that I was wasn't more fun, that I was too reserved and not as available as I could have been, that he didn't *have* more of me.

When he was a little boy, playing in his room or with his friends—this was before play dates were invented—I got things done. That was my programming, after all. Back then, I had Pine-Sol in my veins. I spent too much time cleaning, putting things in order and wiping fingerprints off toasters. I could have been and should have been playing with my only child.

Enter Jack . . . and it's all different now. I'm available, more open and patient. Work is still big in my life, but I have a day just for him. I follow his lead when it comes to play. It's a priority, and he expects it because his parents play with him.

Shawn plays with Jack the way he wanted to be played with at his age. "Just go with whatever he is into at the moment," he says, and "Don't go against the grain." It's incredible for me to see, and I'm very, very proud.

Jack's imagination and creative energy astound me. He was four, and after the carnival came to town, he decided to build one in my kitchen. He got to work on things quickly and before I knew it, my house was dismantled.

First, he asked for permission to use one or two kitchen utensils, and then it was carte blanche and the momentum grew. His ideas were lightning fast. My yoga mats were unrolled and became the carnival walkways, throw pillows were walls, blankets were oceans, and dining room chairs his pirate ship.

Next, he was a shopkeeper in my pantry. Half his toy box was for sale. Boxes of my herbal teas that I had neatly stacked in a basket were all over the floor and in more than one room; bags of pasta were mixed with baking supplies and rolls of tin foil. I made signs for his sale items, but one very important thing was missing.

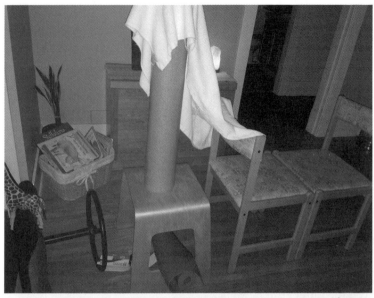

"Buba, we need to set up a little silver bowl so people could tap on it so I know they're there and can come into my shop. I have pirate and viking gear for sale cuz I don't use it anymore."

As I stepped over the mess we'd made and look for a little silver bowl, I saw all my pots and pans in the living room where earlier we'd had a camp fire. This was playing havoc with my insides, and I started to sing the clean-up song. I sang alone.

At three and a half, he liked mending and fixing things, including Buba. "I think your brain is not feeling good, Buba. I need to spit on this, and then put the spit on you. Oh, this bit might hurt." He spit on the hammer in his toolkit and then pressed it deeply into my head and completed this intricate procedure with a little whack to the other side.

"Buba, let's pretend you're a piranha and this [apple on a stick] is a person what shoots rays out . . . " This one didn't turn out well for Buba either, but it was a short game.

At four and five Jack loves experimenting and making mixtures. Buba, not so much. "Buba, could I have a glass of milk, a towel on the table, a tissue, and an old tennis racket would be good. I'm doing an experiment."

"*What?* Where do you do experiments, Jack?"

"At home with Mum and Dad, but this is the first time with milk and stuff."

Oy.

Mixtures are anything Jack thinks would be fun to combine in a bowl. Again—Buba, not so much.

It will take days of soaking and three or four times through the dishwasher before my bowls are ever clean again. And then I heard, "It's a gummy wonderland in here!" Same bowl, different story.

"Here's your crown, Buba. We need a queen in the game." And *we* meant he and I. We're equals when we play.

I value fun, and laughing is part of that—it's when our hearts are fully engaged and we are being who we really are. Jack loves when I am silly and spontaneous. "Buba, can you say something funny again without noticing?"

No more settling down.

The magic of make-believe

Jack, ages 3, 4, and 5

Jack's brilliance amazes me. He is still full of the stardust he came from. I think he captured it best himself when, at four years old, he told me he had a whole cinema in his head. He is never far from magical make-believe moments like these:

He was three. We were at my kitchen sink washing his hands. He was on a small stool, I was behind him, and he said, "It looks like I'm standing, Buba, but I'm actually flying." And you know, I was, too. I remembered a magical moment from my childhood, where I was running and running and running, and then my body gently lifted off the ground, and I was flying high above the fields near my grandparents' home. We stood there, washing hands and flying.

Four-year-old Jack loved to plan and prepare for dinners, special events, and birthday parties. He was very good at it. He also liked and knew a lot about dinosaurs. This is what happens when dinosaurs come to your party:

"T. rexes live in my basement, Buba, and they like to eat eyeballs. I'm inviting them to my party tomorrow. The party is at one o'clock in the afternoon. Come right after you finish lunch, Buba. You have to dress up as a T. rex, Buba, so they don't eat your eyeballs. Then we'll throw the bowls off the table, Buba, and the T. rexes will lick the bowls clean."

Jack was playing with his tool kit, and out came this fascinating and powerful story: "My house tumbled down. It was old, and when I came home from the supermarket, I had no place to put my groceries. I was just forty at the time [he's actually four] and I became a builder. I need all these cards, Buba, because very, very good builders get to give out these cards, Buba. I got them from your drawer."

The next morning, when I went to greet my client, I noticed he had printed "Jack" on one of my business cards.

Jack has a toy box in our living room. It must be magical because it can be a race car, a pirate ship, or a rocket. This day, it was a rocket ship, and three-year-old astronaut Jack was leaving at nine o'clock.

"Buba, will you draw a rocket ship on my hand and write 'Leaving tomorrow at nine o'clock at night'? I can't wait until this is happening. It's so fun! It's my rocket ship, Buba, so I know what buttons to press. That's all I do in my rocket ship. I sit there

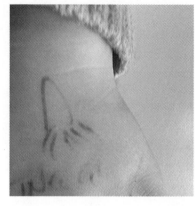

and press buttons. When you see fire in the sky, that will be my rocket ship, Buba. That will be me shooting fire."

I said, "Oh, I love you, Jack!" And he said, "I love you to eleventy hundred universes and back, Buba. Where does the universe stop?"

"I don't know, Jack."

"I'll ask my alien friends and tell you, Buba."

What was I saying about stardust?

At five, Jack liked to hear stories about Granny's, Pop Pop's, Grandpa's, and Buba's childhoods. This is a five-year-old Buba story:

It was the most beautiful, sunny, warm spring day. My buba, I called her Bub for short, was working in her garden, and I was playing by myself. I wished, more than anything, that my friend Katie could be with me, but she was quite a bit older than me and already in school.

Then, all of a sudden, I got the biggest and best idea I'd ever had in my life. I knew how I could make Katie come home. I knew all the kids came home from school on the bus at 3:00. So I pushed a stool up to the kitchen counter and reached the clock on the wall. I moved the hands on the clock and changed the time to 3:00.

I was so excited. I knew this was going to work. I took my stool outside and waited for Katie to come walking up the road. Katie didn't come, but my grandmother did. She walked into the house and said, "Oh, it's after three already? I haven't even seen the school bus go by."

I proudly told her what I'd done to make Katie come home and play with me. She laughed and laughed, and held me close, and told me that's not how it works.

I still have those five-year-old a-ha moments when I think I'm onto a brilliant solution.

The hard part

Jack is teaching me a song about a rat-a-
tatting woodpecker. When I don't get the
words right, he says, "Keep rat-a-tatting,
Buba. I'll do the hard part."

Jack, age 4

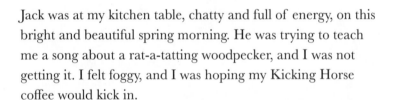

Jack was at my kitchen table, chatty and full of energy, on this
bright and beautiful spring morning. He was trying to teach
me a song about a rat-a-tatting woodpecker, and I was not
getting it. I felt foggy, and I was hoping my Kicking Horse
coffee would kick in.

Sometimes it's funny when I'm being silly. It's a great way for us
to start our day together. In this moment, though, I wasn't fully
present, and I think Jack sensed his buba was a bit off.

I was preoccupied. It wasn't fair. Tuesdays are meant for me
and Jack. Everyone in my life knows this. But this day, my brain
was chugging and too full to focus completely on what's most
important and right in front of me.

Tuesdays with Jack are sacred. On my kitchen cupboard door, I have a list of 12 Zen Things to remind me to be mindful.

When I read the list, it makes complete and utter sense to me. My body feels and understands the truth in each of the twelve things. I know this is the way I want to Be more of the time. Doing things slowly and deliberately, doing less, and putting space between things. This feels like living from the centre of my being.

Honestly, though, I have yet to master number one: Do One Thing at a Time. And I wonder, *Should* a woman do this? *Can* we? What would happen to all the pieces we juggle? Would they land softly and take care of themselves?

My preference and my programming is to see the big picture, multi-task, and take care of it all. In the world of work, I've been rewarded for this. At home, my husband can't take it in, and I overwhelm him. He and my son do one thing at a time, and when Jack is absorbed in something, he doesn't answer me. Is this Zen or simply male?

I think I'm ready to explore this now. It feels like a giant letting-go to get to one thing at a time. Before the fast-forward button came along, I could watch a movie, do housework, get dinner started, and organize my family's next day while the commercials were on. Now I am forced just to watch the movie and *think* about my to-do list.

Maybe the Zen Things were written for a Zen monk. I have a rat-a-tatting four-year-old reminding me to Do One Thing at a Time right now.

Zen Things

1. Do one thing at a time

2. Do it slowly and deliberately

3. Do it completely

4. Do less

5. Put space between things

6. Develop rituals

7. Designate time for certain things

8. Devote time to sitting

9. Smile and serve others

10. Make cleaning and cooking become meditation

11. Think about what is necessary

12. Live simply

Brilliant Little Being

Darndest things

Jack, age 6 months to 5 years

I can hardly remember a time that Jack wasn't talking and on the move. I have a photo of him at six months old, looking very pleased to be standing and peering over the side of his crib, still wearing his sleep sack. That must have felt like quite an accomplishment to stand up in. He crawled at seven months and was walking before he turned a year old. He talked early and hasn't stopped since.

Jack turned two in March. On a Tuesday that June, he and I were walking to the park with my friend Jan. She wanted to get to know him and had a basket of juicy, ripe organic strawberries ready for him. He loved them.

When we arrived at the park, Jack and I were off to the potty. I said, "Isn't Jan a nice lady?" And he answered with, "You're a good woman too, Buba, and I'm a nice boy."

What just happened here? I was stunned. Who would believe a two-year-old toddler would say something like that? He was just out of diapers. His thoughts were crystal clear. And he said *woman*, not *lady*, like I did (appealing to my feminist side).

I won't easily forget the impact Jack had on me that day. It's when I knew he was a brilliant little being, and I started writing down the things he said when we were together. I also wondered how on earth I was going to keep up with this boy. All of my brain cells need to be firing all the time.

I needed a witness, and I was happy I could share what Jack just said with Jan. She was a teacher for many years and agreed that being this boy's buba was going to be very special indeed.

Jack is good company. He's an interesting little person who likes to talk as much as I do. Holding hands, walking, and talking is one of my favourite things to do with him. Unless of course he would prefer to be carried, and then he just goes limp wherever we are.

It was a warm autumn day, and three-year-old Jack and
I were on a walk, getting to know my new neighbourhood.
He never runs out of things to say. I asked him how he knew
so much. And he said, "My brain just tells me, Buba." I stop
and kiss his face.

At times like this, my heart is open, and it is cause for
celebration. The Creator must be sending beautiful and
brilliant beings into this world. You may have one, too.
We need them.

We'd just had lunch out and were on our way back to the car to
go to gymnastics. Jack had to poo, and we were nowhere near a
bathroom. "That's okay, Buba, I can hold it," said four-year-old
Jack. "My bum just sent a message to my brain. I have dinosaur
and human body books. I know a lot about the human body."

One morning I had a little five-year-old wizard in the back
seat of my car. He was wearing his robe and glasses, and
his thick, messy hair just covered the jagged red scar on his

forehead. He made sure his wand and broomstick were right beside him. All was well.

It was a lovely start to Buba Day (that's what Tuesdays are)—Jack had just gotten back from a recent trip to England to visit his family. So his Harry Potter robe was extra special because it was bought there.

His mum painted on his perfect lightning-bolt scar, and his dad's meticulous calligraphy changed Jack's old broom into a flying Nimbus 2000. The round glasses make him look absolutely adorable, and of course he has the accent. He is the perfect Potter.

We were driving to my house. He was not quite as chatty. I rounded a corner and I heard, "Buba, people like you make the brooms, and people like me make them magic."

Whoa. I wasn't sure what Harry Potter book Jack was into now, or why he chose to share that line with me. I felt it. For him, it was gone in a moment. For me, it lingered.

Jack was Harry Potter all day long. At our local co-op grocery store, the staff noticed and engaged to make it even more fun. It was a big deal that Harry Potter was shopping with his buba.

The same wonderful conversations happened at our favourite bakery. There was a man at the counter paying for his food and Jack said, "Buba, he hasn't noticed I'm Harry Potter." And then he did, and talked to Jack like they were old friends. He lit up, and Jack lit up, and it felt like a Hogwarts reunion.

At the park, Jack's robe billowed as he ran around. It got in the way of climbing up ladders and sliding down slides, but he wouldn't take it off. And he still had the round glasses on, too. I guard his wand and broom.

There's a huge checkerboard at the park and Jack wanted us to play, but a grandfather and his two grandchildren were already playing, so we watched on the sideline and waited for our turn. The kids were staring at Jack and they weren't quite sure what to make of him in his costume. I didn't want Jack to feel uncomfortable or teased, so I started thinking maybe he and I should do something else. Just then, the grandfather noticed and invited "Harry Potter" to play too. He talks to Jack as if he was Harry Potter. Brilliant move.

And it just got better. After checkers, Grandpa Dave and his grandchildren included us in a game of catch. Harry Potter fits right in.

It was almost time to leave, Jack with a new group of kids and me chatting with my friend Bradley. I shared Jack's line from this morning's car ride. Bradley went silent, and his eyes were wide. I could see this affected him, too.

Jack made magic for everyone this day.

Jack was almost four when I gave him kinetic sand for Christmas. We loved its soft and silky feel and the way it flows through your hands like thick liquid. I think it moves like brown sugar. And yet we can make castles and mountains with it, too.

Jack's appreciation was precious, and he said, "It falls apart like this, Buba, because there's something magic in it. If we don't protect it, it won't be this anymore." He shows me his spirit in these gems.

I knew there were endless possibilities here. I tried to match words to my feelings and express them in a teachable moment that he would remember forever. I was moved and taken with his sense of knowing, seeing the bigger picture, using the word *protect*, and staying present with him in the all-important Now.

Too late. While Buba's brain was churning, Jack took one of his swords and demolished what we had just built. Kinetic sand was everywhere, and the special magic it contained was now in my vacuum cleaner.

Not quite the lesson I was going for.

The stories we tell ourselves

"I know they're not real, Buba, but I'm scared anyway."

"I know it's not true, but I think there are zombies in Grandpa's closet."

Jack, age 4

I grew up with way too many fears and silly cultural superstitions. I think I was in my forties before I realized that they ruled me. How sad is that?

The biggest reason for my childhood fear is that my mother was often ill, and no one told me what was going on, or how long it would take for her to get better. My greatest fear was that she wouldn't.

Visiting my mother in hospital made me feel nervous because I didn't know what to expect. And that never went away. My mom suffered physically and emotionally. One time there could be tubes and machines attached to her, and the next we would be travelling by train to a special clinic to visit. I remember the fear and the hushed voices. It was no accident she was a nurse, and in between bouts of illness, my mom was one tough cookie.

When she was sick, I was with my grandmother, just the two of us. She was tough in her own way. She could chase a bear out of the yard, making noise with a wooden spoon and wash tub, but in a thunder and lightning storm, she fell apart.

My grandmother was also steeped in superstitions. The one I remember most is this: if a bird hits your window, there will be a death.

Can you imagine what happened when a bird actually flew into my house and perched itself on a tapestry on my wall?

It was a beautiful, sunny summer day. I had just finished cleaning, polishing, and making every room in my dream house spic and span. The door to my balcony is wide open, and my daughter-friend Tammy and I are visiting at my kitchen table over pots of coffee and ashtrays full of cigarettes. (A good time back then.)

Tammy knew me very well. She was looking at me and watching the bird fly around the room, wondering what to do next, because it was up to her to save me and the bird. It didn't take me long to barricade myself in the bathroom, on another floor, until the bird flew away or one of us died.

I heard her talking to the little bird and checking in with me: "Are you okay, Paul?" I also heard loud banging and things falling and I wondered if she was jumping on the furniture to reach the bird.

Finally, it was over. I could come out now. Tammy had taken the lid to an electric frypan (remember those?) and captured the bird, soothed it, and helped it fly free. We collapse into heaps of laughter, relieved we are both alive and the bird is safe.

Not one of my prouder moments (so I think I'll share it in a book). It was ridiculous, and part of me knew. I let my fear totally take over.

At four, Jack had this figured out. When Shawn was four and watching TV, he would ask, "Is this real or pretend?" It was usually when something scary or supernatural came on the screen. Shawn's dad gave clear, simple, scientific answers that he was happy with, and he's now doing the same for Jack.

I wish someone had had the foresight to help me make sense of things when I was four. It's how my OMGs and What Ifs started and grew.

Becoming super

Jack, age 3

Jack hasn't been raised with TV, yet at three he knew all about superheroes and their special powers. Like the added boost he got when he wore his Superman underwear on top of his fastest running shorts. We were at the park, and he was totally comfortable with the look. Not even remotely conscious of what others might think or say.

When my son was three, he wanted to be Yoda at Hallowe'en. I dyed a pair of white tights green to match his little green hoodie and Yoda face mask. He was the most adorable Yoda, and we drove all that day so he could trick-or-treat at my grandparents' house.

He loved those tights. They were very, very special to him, and they kept stretching to fit as he grew. He would even wear them as fun long underwear on cold days.

One day, in his excitement, he decided to show and tell his older best friend all about his Yoda tights. His best friend betrayed him by teasing and mocking him. His little heart broke, and so did mine. That double heartbreak came up for me as I saw Jack being Superman, and I wanted to protect him (and me from triple heartbreak).

I resisted that fearful urge and paid more attention to my joy. Jack didn't need protecting. He felt good about himself, and he told me very clearly, "I'm so Superman, Buba. I'm just not wearing the right shirt. Superman's not a normal guy, Buba."

Now *that's* a superhero!

At the bottom of the basement stairs at my grandparents' house, nine-year-old me wrote *Pauline Connie* in big loopy letters with circles over the i's. I wrote it on the walls and in my schoolbooks, too.

My teacher was not happy with my fancy letters. This is not the way I was taught to write. And *Pauline Connie* is not my name. I just wanted it to be.

All my girlfriends had middle names, and I wished Connie could be mine. My mother gave a middle name to my brother but not to me. When I asked her about it, she blamed my father and told me she liked the name Connie but he'd put Pauline on my birth certificate.

And . . . my Russian last name had nine letters in it. Quite a handle for a shy, skinny little girl. The kids in the small-town school I went to teased, mocked, and shamed me for it. It was awfully cruel, and I was so much happier in a country school with other Russian kids when I moved permanently to my grandparents'.

As I grew, I couldn't wait to get married and change my name, and I did, more than once. When my marriage to Shawn's dad ended, I no longer wanted to share his last name, and I certainly didn't want to go back to my father's. It was time for my own name and identity.

After twenty years of focusing on my husband and son, I don't think I knew what my favourite colour was, and I second-guessed all the decisions I had to make on my own. I paid an eclectic team of tarot card readers, numerologists, and an astrologer who made house calls to tell me I had a future. They, and my vision board, helped me trust myself and grow a backbone.

And then in my office at work just a few weeks later, it came to me—*whoosh*—like a cartoon thought bubble. *Pauline Daniels*, it said. I loved it immediately and called my numerologist to make sure it was a fit. "Drop the S and it's perfect," he said. I checked with my lawyer and she said, "Yes, if you're thinking of changing your name, this is the perfect time."

When my son was nine, he loved the movie *Stand by Me* and the young actor Wil Wheaton. He watched the movie so many

times, he knew most of the dialogue. And for a little while,
I noticed *Wil* written on his schoolbooks with a big loopy W.

Three-year-old Jack had a very distinct superhero name. How
it came to him is a mystery to me. On this day, it's important to
him that I know and remember it: "Say it with me, Buba:
Subaru-Mike-Rocket Ship-Capitol."

I wonder what a numerologist would say about that.

Superheroes and their powers have captured Jack's imagination.
When his dad asked him what he'd do if he had superpowers,
he answered, "I'd run fast and have big hands." In his costume
box, he actually has big green Hulk hands, and they are so
powerful that all he has to do is think of them and he can lift
his fully loaded wheelbarrow and help Grandpa in the yard.

Jack has come to my rescue with his powers, too. One sunny Tuesday, I was having a time scooping hard ice cream into a bowl for him. And then I heard the cutest confident three-year-old voice say, "Let me try, Buba. My muscles are as strong as Wolverine's claws."

The closest I've come to having superpowers was in the early '80s when I was prescribed the corticosteroid prednisone for a medical condition. Shawn was only four, and it was an uncertain and scary time for me. The drug made me gain weight and break out in pimples. Thankfully, it was only for a few weeks.

It also gave me *energy*. I could go, go, go and do, do, do and needed very little sleep. That part was good and suited my nature then. When I shared this with my doctor, he thought it was a good thing I could only get the drug through prescription.

We were renting our home at the time and shared a wall with a neighbour who loved to play music very loud. One day something just snapped (I understand that term now), and I had had enough. I spun around and kicked the wall. It felt like one of those spinning, high karate kicks from the hip.

My foot went right through the wall. I was shocked and couldn't believe what I had just done. Shawn, on the other hand, was so impressed with my stunning manoeuvre, he said, "Just like Wonder Woman, Mom!"

When Jack tells me about his superpowers, he's very clear. He knows how they help him and when they're there, and he can feel them in his blood. "Superpowers creeped out a little hole [above his knee] and they help me walk," he told me. "I can feel when they are there and when they're not. I can feel it in my blood because that's where my superpowers are."

This amazes me. I don't know where it comes from. Maybe he's heard or seen it in a comic book. It feels like a deep inner knowing coming from a little person.

I hope he carries this with him forever. It makes much more sense than Buba's karate-kickin' ways.

Hi-yah!

Laughter

Jack, age 18 months to 5 years

I love laughing. It's one of my favourite things to do and how I want to be remembered. Laughing is an expression of my love and the sound of my joy.

In a beautiful Sufi tale of creation that I heard, laughter is elevated and celebrated because it keeps the body and soul in harmony. Can't you just feel the ultimate truth in that? Laughter is more than a gift, it's a sacred responsibility. It's divine music, and the world needs more.

I laugh easily and often. Most people appreciate it, others are bugged by it, and some misunderstand it. Laughter is a huge connector, and mine has been misinterpreted as flirting (I'm not, I'm just laughing), being disrespectful (I hope not), or a hiding place (well, sometimes).

Laughing has also got me into heaps of trouble, because I can go from zero to bizarre in a nanosecond with the right person, and they are everywhere. My brother has always been one of those people. (It's a Robin Williams kind of thing.) We can laugh uncontrollably, and we think we are hysterically funny. Not everyone agrees with us, and we feel for them.

Laughter is many things—most of all, it's pure and it's special. One day at our favourite bakery, where we have lovely conversations and the best treats, three-year-old Jack asked me a deep, rich question that I was not prepared for:

"Do you laugh when I'm not with you, Buba?"

This took my breath away. It was another holy moment with this child, and my Tuesdays are filled with them.

"I do, but laughing when I'm with you, my sweetheart, is the best thing in the whole . . . wide . . . world!" He has my heart and soul and he knows it.

Unless my gloves are attached to a string around my neck, I lose a pair every year. I don't know why. I had been hoping to break this pattern with my latest purchase. But just as they were starting to feel buttery soft, one went missing.

I searched everywhere, becoming more and more upset with myself. Feeling immature and irresponsible, hearing my mother's words: "You'd lose your head if it wasn't screwed on." Well, there you go, that's probably my why.

And then I stopped my frantic search and asked my team of angels to help me find my glove. Ding! I remembered and saw them clearly, lying right where I had left them. I called, and sure enough, my glove was still there.

The next day, picking up my glove was at the top of my to-do list. It was a sunny, chilly winter day, and five-year-old Jack was with us as we were out and about doing errands. I was so happy to have my glove back. I said, "This makes my day!"

And from the backseat I heard, "I make your day, Buba."

He's right. He knows how precious and important he is to me, and he knows how to make me laugh. We are all laughing. It feels like a celebration of being seen, heard, and appreciated.

"Eeek! Just dropped Jack off for his first sleepover! Our first night ever apart, it's going to be strange but SO nice to sleep in in the morning. Thanks, Pauline and Jim."

Jack's mum's Facebook post on New Year's Eve 2012. Jack was just over eighteen months old, and he's been with me every New Year's Eve since.

"Hey, Jack, do you want a sleepover on Friday?"

"Of course, why wouldn't I?"

He's five and we try to have a sleepover at least once a month. It gives his parents a date night, and gives Jack and me time to visit and stay connected—especially now that he's in school.

It's pretty good at Buba's. And that's the way it's supposed to be. He has his favourite food, all the dessert he can eat, and now that he's older, a movie or two. He is my special little guest.

When Jack was a toddler, he'd wake, peer over his portable playpen and say, "Buba, I'm all done." Then it was, "Is it morning time, Buba?" Now he tells time and says, "Hi, Buba, it's time to get up."

Jack sleeps right beside my bed. When he could climb out of his playpen, his mum found a child's inflatable plastic bed that I bought with my grocery shopping points. It was a good idea in theory, but the smell of the plastic was so strong. The label said it didn't contain anything harmful, but it filled the room with a strange new-car smell. When we cuddled up together, it squeaked and groaned and threw me right off the side. It wasn't a Buba-friendly bed.

A trunk full of my grandmother's homemade wool quilts, folded in two and piled high, make a soft, warm, cozy bed big enough for both of us to stretch out, read, cuddle up, and fall asleep on. We both think it's a bit like the princess and the pea.

I was lucky enough to go on the long day trips we took for my grandmother to buy her wool. I remember her washing it, hanging it on the line, and carding it by hand before making it into sturdy quilts with bright, patterned covers.

I've had them for years, and I know that the energy and love that went into making them surrounds Jack as he sleeps over.

>Jack's parents send him a selfie and let him know that they are on the way to pick him up. He kisses the phone.

>*Jack, age 5*

Jack was in my arms, cuddled up with a book, a blanket, and some snacks. It was the end of our day and almost time for his mum and dad to pick him up.

Shawn and Chloe were running a bit late and sent him a selfie to say they were now on their way. He kissed the phone. I wanted to cry. That happens a lot now.

In this moment of tenderness and love, my heart knew how fortunate Jack was and how proud I was of his parents. I have nothing to worry about as his buba.

Jack's is a close family. When I was five, I was still an only child. I couldn't trust my parents to care for me in the way that Jack's mum and dad care for him. And we lived in Vancouver at the time, far from my grandparents, who were sick with worry.

Somehow, my mother thought it would be a good idea for my father to take me to see *Bambi* at the local theatre. Back then, it was going to the picture show. During the hour we were there, my father managed to get drunk and bring me home wearing only one winter boot. To this day, hearing or seeing an image of Bambi or a small fawn or Thumper the rabbit makes me feel sad and empty. I would *not* take a child to see that movie.

This is a pitiful and painful memory to revisit; it's what comes up as I write. I share it because I don't believe that children are as resilient as we think they are, and that way of thinking may be an excuse to ignore the real damage done to them.

I could never understand why even the tiniest sip of apple juice made my entire body want to double over with an emotion I had no language for. One day, I shared this with my mother, who immediately gave me the answer. "Of course. It's what they fed you in the hospital."

This mild experience is an example of how important it is to explain things to children, to talk, connect, and tie up loose ends. So many of us live with deep wounds and scars, and deeply wound others.

Love, loyalty, and a solid foundation are the building blocks for resilience in life. If we were resilient as children, our world would be a very different place.

"Skipping is the fastest way to get around, Buba."

Jack, age 5

When was the last time you skipped down a sidewalk, street, dirt road, or anywhere?

I've had to start skipping to keep up with Jack. He skips everywhere, including the mall, the park, the grocery store, and through my house. He loves it, and tells me it's the fastest way to get around.

As I skip down the street with Jack, I'm awkward and unsure of myself. I can't remember the last time I did this. I hope it comes back to me soon. I have visions of myself tripping or getting tangled in my own feet, then falling in a heap on the street, and as I lift my bleeding face, Jack keeps skipping farther and farther away from me.

I lumber and lurch along, and it reminds me of the jumping at the gym. The first time my trainer asked me to jump onto a step, I just stood there with a blank look on my face while others were leaping like gazelles. I couldn't make my body jump. The signal in my brain for jumping had vanished. It took guts and practice for me to learn to jump again.

I was happy skipping came back faster than jumping, and with less trauma. It took a few tries to get the hippity-hop from-foot-to-foot action going smoothly, and I wanted to feel carefree and joyous like Jack. His body spontaneously catches the feeling and off he goes. I'm not there yet.

Jack leads. He's fast and agile. I feel too big, clumsy, and uncomfortable in my body for skipping down the street. This is not new. It's about me being klutzy. Something I've never outgrown.

And I can't skip over it.

Lessons

Listen and learn

Sitting on my swing, reading and talking.
"You learn so quickly, Jack."
"You do too, Buba."

Jack, age 3

Sitting on my swing, on a warm summer day, is one of my favourite things to do. It's calm and peaceful, and I'm not. A naturopathic doctor once described me as having two speeds— full speed ahead or stop. My swing is an in-between place, like third gear.

It's a little retreat in my backyard. And it evokes a special memory of a poem my mom read to me from *A Child's Garden of Verses*. It was "The Swing," and I loved everything about it. The picture of the little girl "up in the air so blue," my mom's voice as she was reading, and the feelings of fun and freedom it gave me.

Everyone should have a swing. My garden swing is where I first discovered Mike's Hard Lemonade, a magical mix of vodka, natural flavours, and carbonated water. Perfect summer-time fare for contemplating life, and it's a Canadian company to boot. Patriotic, eh? Just me and my swing and a little buzz. It's okay, it was just a phase, and I wasn't a buba yet.

Seriously though, my grown-up swing is where I let go and just be. I can't imagine summer without one. Add Jack, and it's a whole new dimension. When he was a baby, I'd sing and gently rock and he'd fall asleep beside me. Swing, summer, sleeping grandbaby. How does it get any better?

In my swing, we read piles of books, sing songs, laugh, cuddle up with blankets and soft pillows, eat lunch, talk, and just hang out. We are really together and close in my swing. It's our cozy outdoor base. And we've been doing this since he was tiny.

I am amazed that Jack can sing every word in a song he's heard once at playgroup and remember stories from books he only hears with me. I tell him and give him a great big squeeze.

Back to Jack and me in the swing this day: he knows he can do something better than Buba. My heart melts. There is such a deep caring and inclusion in this moment. He's three. This is a beautiful moment between us. I don't think it would have happened at my kitchen table. It's the swing.

> Oh, I do think it the pleasantest thing
> Ever a child can do!
>
> *Robert Louis Stevenson*

Wah, wah, wah

"Come on, Jack. It's time to clean up before your mum and dad are here to pick you up."

"I can hear, I'm not listening."

Jack, age 4

Ever feel like Charlie Brown's teacher when you talk to your family? "Wah, wah, wah." I do. It's not that I put them to sleep. It's that sometimes I feel they don't really pay attention to me, like background noise.

I wonder, do they care what I think or have to say? Would they like to get to know me before it's too late? I gave my mom a journal one Christmas and asked her to write in it and tell me about her life. She didn't. This is the hard stuff.

Maybe they find me boring and hard to be around like my mother was for me a lot of the time. Oh, I hope not. She would go on and on and on about her operations, her sore back, her doctors, and her friends with illnesses, until over the years my brother and I unconsciously tuned her out. We must have come across like uncaring wretches.

We did the same thing to my grandmother, too, because she exaggerated everything. But it was funny. To get us up and moving for school, she would yell from the bottom of the stairs, "It's after seven o'clock already, get up!" We'd come scrambling down to find it wasn't quite 6:00 a.m. She did this every day.

Perhaps it's just my turn not to be heard. You know, what goes around comes around. Because it happens with my husband, too. I'll say something to him and he'll answer with "What's that you said?" I used to repeat myself until he told me his hearing test was perfect. Hmmmmm . . .

Now, I say it once and wait for my words to catch up to his attention span. Some of our conversations have an odd delay, like a news anchor talking to a reporter on location.

Back in the day, my favourite boss thought I had buckets of common sense and he appreciated it. From this place, I often want to say, "Please listen to me. No one loves you more than I do!" But I hold back for fear of offending. Aren't we all a little afraid of our kids?

When I phoned home, my grandparents would often start the call with "Is everything okay?" or "Is anything wrong?" It finally kicked in that that would stop when I called home more often just to say hello.

Lives can be overly busy—maybe I need to speak faster, or louder. Don't let my common sense, wisdom, or the fact that I've been around a while now fly out the door. Take it while I'm here. Guaranteed you'll miss it.

Jack summed it up perfectly when I asked him to clean up his mess before his parents came to pick him up at the end of the day. He said, "I can hear, I'm not listening."

And there you have it. It takes effort to hear and listen. You have to want to.

Wah, wah, wah.

Who's teaching whom?

Jack, ages 3 and 4

When we moved into our current home, Jack was three and involved from the beginning. We came to the house together a few times, so he knew where Buba was moving, what the yard was like, and where his toy box would be in the new house. Farther away meant a seven-minute drive across town to Buba's rather than a two-minute drive around the corner.

Jack knows that he belongs at Buba's house. It's his second home. That was a missing piece for me as a child. I didn't have a family home. I was taken in by my grandparents. Where did I belong? There's a restlessness that comes from this. Perpetually visiting.

Moving in, organizing, setting up my coaching room and office with Jack around has its challenges. He hides everywhere. When I ask him to be careful not to touch the cords and wires under my desk, he tells me his dad's a plumber and he knows all about touching wires.

I love that! I didn't have those experiences with a dad, and he does. I could never say "my dad" in any meaningful way and in this moment, in his cheeky way, Jack tells me he is loyal to his dad. My boys, my son and his son, have broken patterns.

Jack is also loyal to his family and the way they do things. We were in a hurry one day, and I told him he didn't have to tuck his pants into his boots because there wasn't any snow outside. He's four and corrects me. "We tuck them in in every season, Buba." They are close, a unit.

I'm loyal to my brother.

I like things a particular way, and Jack likes to rearrange them. He made me something at preschool and presented it to me. I placed it very carefully on the windowsill near my desk and told him how special I thought it was, that I would think about him every time saw it.

I thought he was happy that I had placed it carefully in the corner of my windowsill . . . until the next Tuesday when he

was here. He was out of sorts and not happy with me, and he decided to tell me that that beautiful thing he made for me shouldn't balance, Buba, it should hang. I had made a mistake.

I don't know that I ever had that freedom to be so involved in putting things where I thought they should be with my grandmother or my mother. I like that he can be honest and open and tell me what he thinks. Soon he'll be rolling his eyes.

Legacy

How to leave a legacy

"Are you going to write a book about all the funny things I say, Buba?"

"Well, who would read it?"

"Oh, just anybody. I'll sell them at my lemonade stand."

Jack, age 5

Since Jack could talk, I've been writing down some of the brilliant things he says when we are together on Tuesdays. I call these gems Jackisms. Our whipped cream experience was one of the first things I shared on Facebook, and it's how Tuesdays with Jack began.

I couldn't not share these dazzling tidbits. They wanted to jump out of me, too. I was concerned that it could be seen as exploitative. And, most importantly, I didn't want to upset his parents. Their rule was I could share, but no photos.

So, after Jack is gone at the end of the day and my house is sort of put back together, I reread my notes and choose two or three of his treasures to share on my Facebook page. If I miss a Tuesday, readers often send me personal messages reminding me. "Ah, hello, it's Wednesday, wondering what you and Jack were up to yesterday." Or this: "It's Wednesday and there's no Tuesdays with Jack. Your fans are waiting."

I am very happy these sharings are enjoyed and appreciated, because I cherish them. I share them exactly the way Jack says them, including the number of times he says Buba, which is at least fifty on a Tuesday. We live in a small town, and one day a woman walked up to me and said, "Hi, are you Buba?" That was funny, charming, and just lovely.

My friend Helen, who was away receiving treatment for her rare cancer, sent me this message on January 6, 2015: "Just read all the Tuesdays with Jack out loud to John [her husband]. They are even better as spoken word. Thanks for that." Her message moved me to tears and still does.

The people who read my posts are positive, kind, and enthusiastic supporters. Some have encouraged me to do more and actually write a book. It took a long while for the desire to ignite in me. Once it did, it wouldn't go away, and I knew I had to trust it. The summer before Jack started kindergarten, I made my plans to begin.

On a hot day that same summer, not far from their house, Jack and his mum set up a lemonade stand to raise money for MS. It is dear to their hearts because Jack's friend's mother lives with it. The stand was Jack's craft table, and my huge stock pot held the icy lemonade. Buba and Grandpa were two of Jack's first customers.

After a bit, Jack got right into promoting and selling his lemonade. He was bold, pitching his product and flagging down cars to make the sale. In a few hours, he raised $50 for MS. His efforts were recognized, and a photo of him and his lemonade stand made the local MS society newsletter.

I think he may be looking to expand his product line. Watch for *Tuesdays with Jack*, the book, at a lemonade stand near you.

What Buba's house smells like

Kids are here for dinner.
Jack walks in and says,
"It smells good in here!"

Jack, age 5

A whole lot of special happens to me when you tell me it *smells* good in my house. It's an instant feeling of warmth and connection, like a current of appreciation that runs through both of us at exactly the same time.

It's much more than a compliment. It's an embrace. And it lifts me up. When I hear Shawn or Jack tell me, "It smells good in here," something huge happens to my heart. I am sooooo Mom (or sooooo Buba) in that moment.

I also love when people tell me that it *feels* good in my house. It's a genuine energy that you feel and know like a warm blanket, and it goes beyond the placement of things. I've had a bright blue Thomas the Tank Engine toy box in my dining room for a few years. It does nothing for the decor or beauty in my home, and it's probably not good feng shui, but it belongs.

The sense of smell is so powerful. In my family, we all know the smell of Auntie Nada's basement. Or that very special one-of-a-kind smell of Auntie Mable's house. The Old Spice my grandfather wore. Cut-up dill will always mean a pot of borscht is ready.

When Shawn was nine, we bought a new house. Even after I cleaned and disinfected everything, he would ask, "When is it going to smell like ours?" His sweet way of saying he wanted the move to be over and for the new house to be and feel like home.

So important no matter how old we are. I've been in homes where it feels like a family of six could put everything into a big garbage bag and move out in an hour. Other homes make you want to kick your shoes off and curl up with the rest of the family.

It's that peaceful, settled-in feeling that comes with living and loving where you are, and knowing you're not going anywhere any time soon. And if you do, it will smell and feel exactly the same way there . . . *home*.

Portrait in purple

"Buba, for your birthday I want to paint you wearing this [fuzzy purple hoodie] and laughing with lots of sound bubbles."

Jack, age 5

When Jack was two, he and his dad presented me with a painting for my birthday. Shawn's colourful calligraphy letters spelled *Happy Birthday, Buba*. In one corner he drew a cartoon face of Grover from *Sesame Street*, and on the other side Jack painted squiggly lines and poked holes through the canvas with his paintbrush. The effect was stunning.

I love this little painting and have it displayed in my office. That's where we were on this chilly Tuesday, talking about my birthday coming up again in the next few days.

I was wearing my favourite purple hoodie that was a treat to myself a couple of birthdays ago. Jack teased me about "wearing it all the time." How can I not? It's just the right shade of purple, warm, cozy, and fun. It makes me feel good, although I've now learned that the fabric is not environmentally friendly and probably needs to be recycled with my mercury light bulbs.

I was sitting and Jack was standing very close to me: close to my face, almost eye to eye. He was excited, and full of ideas for my birthday. As he shared them with me, he spotted the painting, and he was instantly inspired to paint me another. A portrait this time.

He made a circle in the air with his hands, to indicate he saw me in my purple hoodie (of course), and then he described what he wanted to capture about his buba and how he planned to do that in his painting. It was the most beautiful thing I could hear.

I felt loved and appreciated and totally overcome with joy, tears and laughter. I hurriedly searched for my notepad to write this down before it disappeared.

What a wildly delightful compliment to receive from the little love of my life. That is how I will always remember this day, and how I hope Jack will always remember me.

Gingerbread cookies

"When I'm eleven, Buba, I
will do this with you."

Jack, age 4

Gingerbread is my thing. It's a tradition I started when Shawn
was a little boy. First I made it for him, then we made it
together. And now, I'm doing that with Jack.

It's so much more than a cookie. It's a connection to my little
boy, to my grandfather, to my grandson and to myself.

When my Shawn came along, I went from reading *Cosmo* to
Canadian Living. I think it helped me be a better mom. I love the
name, *Canadian Living*. It's where I learned to cook my first of
many, many Thanksgiving turkeys, bake bread that I didn't grow
up with, be heart smart, and, of course, where my never-fail,
rich and spicy, full-of-love gingerbread recipe came from.

Year after year, I made batch after batch of gingerbread in all
shapes and sizes. When they were ready, I lay them carefully on
bright pink sheets on my kitchen floor, and together Shawn and
I decorated them.

We huddle over the mounds of cookies and bowls of coloured icing in our own little assembly line. Bright green trees, yellow stars, white snowmen, red and white santas, and gingerbread boys and girls. Enough for eating, gifting, and hanging on our tree. The mingling scent of gingerbread and Christmas tree makes every cell in my body feel warm and safe.

Christmas baking was also a way I could show my grandfather I loved him. Only the best gingerbread cookies and mincemeat tarts were meant for him. If we weren't together over the holidays, they were sent on the good old reliable Greyhound bus. He thanked me over and over for his goodies. And I knew exactly where he'd sit to savour his strong black tea and treats.

One year, my gingerbread turned out better than ever, which was great, because my grandfather preferred his without icing. Each cookie was almost perfect, full of love and smelling of Christmas. I packed them gently between layers and layers of wax paper and put them in shoeboxes for safe shipping.

Not such a great idea. When he opened the boxes, the spicy, sweet smell of gingerbread and mince meat was mixed with the overpowering smell, and unfortunately taste, of Italian leather.

A big disappointment for both of us that Christmas. The next year, I bought red and green cookie tins just for him. I am grateful and happy to have had many more years of baking for my grandfather, and I still use those tins. It's the memories and love in them that make my gingerbread even better now.

Jack was about nine months old his first Christmas. I made gingerbread cookies for Shawn and Chloe and a few special little gingerbread men with white icing and sprinkles to hang on their tree. Again, not such a great idea . . .

Shawn was holding baby Jack near their Christmas tree. Then Jack spotted one of the little gingerbread cookies, and he dove out of his father's arms and into the tree to reach it. The tree almost came crashing to the ground. No one was hurt—only a mess to clean up and all the other gingerbread men to take off the tree and hide from Jack. Buba's fault for making the cookies in the first place.

I can hardly believe that I am now making gingerbread with my Jack. He chooses the shapes, and I bake them using the same wonderful recipe. Jack gets the organic version. They are spread out on towels (I miss those pink sheets), and together we ice each cookie, made from organic powdered sugar and natural food colouring. Then he pours sickeningly sweet artificially coloured sprinkles all over them.

When Jack was four, we received brand new cookie cutter shapes from my daughter-friend Tammy. We had gingerbread men and ninjabread men in our cookie tins that year. As we are decorating them, I tell Jack that this is exactly what his dad and I did every Christmas until he was too old to want to anymore. Jack looks at me, thinks about it for a minute, and assures me he will be right here making gingerbread with Buba for a long time yet, or at least until he's eleven.

The wonder of it all

Shawn asked me to listen to the song "7 Years." That made me feel so good, and I was flattered, thinking there was something meaningful in the song he wanted to share with me.

As I was listening and watching it on YouTube, Jack was snuggling on my lap. I realized I knew and liked the song, and sang along to it in my car. It's catchy and stays with you. Now, I was paying careful attention to the lyrics.

Some were popping out for me, and I wondered if these were the meaningful parts for Shawn.

"When I was seven years old, my mama told me . . . "

"I only see my goals, I don't believe in failure . . . "

"Remember life and then your life becomes a better one . . . Soon, I'll be sixty years old, will I think the world is cold?"

You can see I'd painted an extra special moment for myself there. Shawn asked me to listen to this song, his son was on my lap, the tune and some of the lyrics tugged at me, and I was almost sobbing at the beauty of it all.

Some time later I say, "Hey, Shawn, what was the reason you wanted me to listen to that song?"

My heart is open and I'm thinking I'm going to hear that he really loves me and just wanted to share something special with his mom.

"I'm not sure," he says. "Catchy, I think."

"Really, that's it?" I say.

"Yup," he says.

Turns out, this was a special moment for one. But that's okay, I could celebrate it anyway. It's a story about deep love and laughter, and I wish I could share it with my mom and grandmother.

How I miss them. I imagine calling my mom and telling her about this and hearing her laugh. I think of my grandmother, too, who would laugh and then share something equally funny. Just thinking about it makes me feel connected to them now.

My mom's love was iffy growing up, and it was only after I was an adult that I felt more connected to her. Not long ago, something incredible happened while I was sitting at my desk, thinking about work. I felt the strongest feeling of love coming to me. I've never experienced anything like this before. It was exactly the same feeling of love I have for my son and grandson. That's why I knew, in that special moment, it was my mother's love I was receiving.

Seasons, flowers, and laughter remind me of my grandmother. A few years ago, I was running along a trail just after a rain. As I rounded a corner, there was a deep purple lilac bloom with a single drop of rain on it, hanging onto the path, right in front of me. I held it, buried my face in it, and wept.

And in that moment—in the wonder of it all—I knew love is stronger than any separation.

Mom

Epilogue

The things that last

"Can I sit in your lap, Buba?"
"Forever and a day."

Jack, age 4

My son is my one and only. He's the child I was supposed to have. It was a conscious choice I made, but as a mother of an only, parenting always feels new. What I know for sure is that everything about my boy has affected everything about me, from his caretakers to my career path. And it started early.

When he was a baby, I had to leave him for a few days. He was with my mother, who loved him almost as much as I did, and I still cried the entire time I was gone. It was more than a missing. My arms actually felt empty and ached to hold him.

How could I return to work feeling this way? That's when I knew I could only ever leave him with my mom. Her love sustained us both.

A few years later, I was working with some of the brightest minds in the high-powered corporate world and earning a very good income. On the outside it looked and sounded great, but it wasn't me, and I struggled to fit the mold. My boss changed my name to Paul and told me never, ever to cry—which made me want to cry. I was torn every day between my career, my marriage, and my little boy. Have we come a long way, baby?

When my four-year-old sweetheart was almost ready for kindergarten, and on a rare weekend off, he and I did some baking together. Later, I saw him running through our neighbourhood with a cookie held high, proudly telling everyone, "These are homemade!" And in that powerful moment, I knew this is not the way I want to mother and raise my only little boy.

No more budget meetings and late nights.

I willingly gave up my high-heeled shoes, my designer suits, and my generous paycheques for a job that started at 10:00 and ended at 2:00 so I could still support my family and be the mother I wanted to be.

Close to home, I found the perfect place to work, offering me exactly what I wanted with an almost magical connection to the staff and employers. It was fun, we were encouraged to be who we were. I grew with the company, time flew, and I stayed for six years.

When my son was involved in hockey, I loved it. That arena smell of ice, hot dogs, and old wood. It felt great to be part of a community, supporting our kids and making a difference. I was at the arena almost as often as Shawn, and I began thinking it would be wonderful to take this hockey experience into the world of work.

Again, I found meaningful work in my neighbourhood at a counselling centre. I worked with smart, funny, supportive, and deeply caring people. Good thing, because as my new career path began, my twenty-year marriage ended. This wonderful work family helped me through a divorce, single parenting my then-teen son, and returning to school.

My life and career path is a result of the inextricable bond with my son. Something he may not know until now, or might feel with his own son. One of the hardest things I've had to do was leave him, this time to return home after a death in my family. He decided not to make the move, and at nineteen, was on his own. I spent the next year in intense worry and concern over his welfare and well-being. Happily, he joined me shortly after.

Our relationship continues to evolve now that I am mother and grandmother. I am flooded with emotion when I see my son and grandson together. And as Jack sits in my lap, I wish he could stay forever. I call these *Love You Forever* moments, from Robert Munsch's book that I have yet to read without sobbing halfway through.

Now my beautiful boy and his beautiful boy have given me material to write a book. Who knew a grandmother's love and a little boy's brilliance would take me here? The wonder, intensity, thrill, hard work, and the process that touched or came from my soul has propelled me into my third act.

I've actually begun to start sentences with "When I'm gone" or "When I die," and I've asked my son to play "Spirit in the Sky" at my funeral. He nodded and probably didn't know how to process that information. *Did I just hear what Mom said?* I hope this isn't a premonition but a transition into the next phase of my life. It's scary—very real and necessary.

These last five years of Tuesdays with Jack have been utterly delightful, powerful, and poignant. While I adore Jack, it's his dad who will always be my baby.

Thank You

To my Facebook friends who appreciated and understood my need to share the brilliance in Jack's "Jackisms" every Tuesday in my posts.

In particular, Julia Gillmor, who recognized the genius in Jack's nuggets and encouraged me to actually *do* something with them. Thank you!

To Kendall McPherson, who saw Tuesdays with Jack as a love story and told me these treasures needed to be in a book. I am grateful for your faith in me.

To my husband Jim, who supported me every step of the way. His photos capture magic.

About the Author

Pauline Daniel loves being a grandmother. She describes herself as a Baby Boomer Buba and like most things of her generation—it's big in her life.

This book began as a Facebook post every Tuesday after spending the day with her grandson, Jack. Tuesdays have been their day since he was a baby. When he started talking, he came out with the most brilliant, articulate and imaginative queries and comments. She *had* to share them.

Before long, *Tuesdays with Jack* had a following. Her readers suggested she should share the stories with the world. On the day Jack went to Kindergarten, Pauline started to write. It came together in this little book.

In addition to being a first-time author, Pauline Daniel is the owner of Coaching Connections, a life-coaching practice, serving women. She calls herself the *How to Follow Your Heart* Coach, which is the way she lives her life.

Pauline and her husband Jim live in a small town in British Columbia. Jack and his family live nearby.